CARNIVAL ROUND THE CENTRAL FIGURE

Diana Amsterdam

BROADWAY PLAY PUBLISHING INC
224 E 62nd St, NY NY 10065-8201
212 772-8334 fax: 212 772-8358
BroadwayPlayPubl.com

CARNIVAL ROUND THE CENTRAL FIGURE
© Copyright 2011 by Diana Amsterdam

First printing: October 2011
Second printing: May 2012
I S B N: 978-0-88145-504-5

Book design: Marie Donovan
Page make-up: Adobe Indesign
Typeface: Palatino
Printed and bound in the U S A

ABOUT THE AUTHOR

Diana Amsterdam's new play, CARNIVAL ROUND THE CENTRAL FIGURE, was produced at Kori Rushton's I R T Theater in New York's West Village in January 2011, where it was highly praised and received a glowing review from *The New York Times*.

Amsterdam's plays have been developed or produced by M C C, Soho Rep, Atlantic Theater Company, Abingdon Theater Company, American Stage Company, Cucaracha, New York Theater Workshop, and Kori Rushton's I R T Theater.

Amsterdam wrote her first play in 1990. It was produced that same year at Paul Sorvino's American Stage Company in Teaneck, NJ. That play was FAST GIRLS, since published by Samuel French, the recipient of a Hugo in Montreal (that city's equivalent of a Tony) and commissioned by the B B C.

Amsterdam is a New York State Council on the Arts grant recipient, winner of the B B C American Radio Play Contest, winner of a Hugo Award (Montreal) for Best Comedy, Producers Choice for Best in Festival at the Source in Washington DC, and award-winner New Millennium Writings and New Century Writers. Her play MILK was selected for H B O's Stage to Screen Series.

She is much published: FAST GIRLS and SEX AND DEATH by Samuel French; BEAUTIFUL CLEAR-

EYED WOMAN and IKEN'S PERVERSION by Playscripts. She is widely published in one-act, scene and monologue anthologies from Saint Martins Press, Applause Books and Smith & Kraus. Her work is often included in college curricula.

From the published works, her plays are produced around the world, and her radio plays FAST GIRLS, DINNER AT THE GOTHAM BAR AND GRILL and CRAZY LUCK are broadcast in England, Germany and Wales.

Diana's screenplay *The Love Hit* is optioned to John E Ferraro, formerly a Paramount executive, now independent producer and manager. Her romantic comedy *The Other Woman* won first prize in New York Women and Film's 25th Anniversary Screenplay Contest. Diana is writing a new screenplay, *World's Worst Lover*.

Diana is represented for theater by Jonathan Mills at Paradigm (212-897-6400) and for film and T V by John E Ferraro of Los Angeles (323-428-3042).

CARNIVAL ROUND THE CENTRAL FIGURE had its New York premiere at I R T Theater (Producer, Kori Rushton; Managing Producer, Jaki Silver) in the West Village of New York City on 17 January 2011. The cast and creative contributors were:

THE CENTRAL FIGURE .... Ted Caine
KATE .... Danni Simon
RICHARD .... Ed Stelz
SHEILA .... Christine Rowan
MARYANNE .... Livia Scott
JOHN TUPPER .... David Michael Kirby
BECKY TUPPER .... Cynthia Silver
THE PREACHER .... Shane LeCocq
NURSE .... Kori Rushton
CHOIR .... Stephanie Hsu, Brandon Kyle Goodman,
            Janna Emig, Rebecca Schoffer, Raymond Hill,
                                             & Carla Briscoe
THE FOUR PEOPLE .... Stephanie Hsu, Brandon Kyle
            Goodman, Raymond Hill, Christine Rowan
VOICE OF FRANKY JACK .... John Early

Director .... Karen Kohlhaas
Assistant director .... Arden Walentowsky
Stage manager .... Veronica Graveline
Lighting design & tech direction .... Eric Southern
Music director .... David James Boyd
Scenic design .... Walt Spangler with Jisun Kim &
                                             Melissa Shakun
Choreography .... Karen Kohlhaas & Shane Lecocq
Master carpenter .... Matt Vieira
Logo design .... Dylan Sanford

Graphic design .... Kaveh Haerian
Photography .... Deneka Peniston
Public relations .... Springer Assoc's, Joe Trentacosta

CHARACTERS

KATE, *mid 20s*
RICHARD, KATE's *boyfriend, mid 20s*
SHEILA, *mid 30s—Paul's [*CENTRAL FIGURE/CF*], wife*
MARYANNE, *40s—a hospital psychologist*
JOHN, *late 30s*
BECKY, *late 30s*
THE NURSE, *ageless*
THE PREACHER, *any age*

THE CHOIR—*all ages or any age. At least 3 people; up to 20*

THE FOUR PEOPLE—*may double-cast with* CHOIR; *one is* SHEILA

THE CENTRAL FIGURE, CF *is beyond gender, age, and most other distinguishing features. CF is grotesque: inhumanly thin, ghastly pale, and bald. CF is perpetually concentrating on something of life-and-death importance; this extreme concentration contorts CF's face into uncivilized expressions. Eyes dart wildly, focusing on nothing; hands fly over the sheets like captured butterflies, picking at the cloth, bunching it, rubbing it; limbs occasionally go into a tremor or convulsion.*
CF *wears a thin hospital gown.*
When CF responds to something external, it is like a dreamer responding to a faraway, perhaps ominous, sound.

THE SETTING

A wide open space, in the center of which is a hospital bed. In the bed lies the Central Figure. His bed is accentuated: raised, or tipped toward the audience. A T V is referred to in the play, as are bananas, finger rings and other props; having these on stage, or not, is the decision of the director. There may be hiding space under the bed from which The Four People chillingly emerge.

The Nurse is on stage at all times. She is accentuated in some way: on a pedestal, or framed by hospital scrims.

A Powerpoint presentation and slide show are part of the show. There is a raised screen upon which to project these.

THE MOOD OF THE PLAY

There is a three-ring circus quality to the action. The play should be surprising, upsetting, hilarious, noisy, colorful, sensual and musical.

INTERMISSION

The play may run with our without an intermission.

ON THE NONLINEAR TIME PROGRESSION

This play is a story told through the viewpoint of Kate, the protagonist. The "actual" real-time, here & now scenes are the core of the story. These are the four scenes at Paul's hospital bedside that include Kate,

Richard, Sheila and later Maryanne. In these scenes, the Central Figure is the 37-year-old man, Paul.

In other scenes, the Central Figure is the 16-year-old girl, Pamela Tupper. The part should be played the same for both personages of the Central Figure.

The play jumps around in time and space. We see Kate's memory scenes, exaggerated by fear and youth, of her encounter, and the Tuppers's T V encounters, with the Preacher fifteen years ago.

We also see Kate's nightmares. These feature the Four People, who should be darkly funny and also sinister and frightening.

The play is a memory play: only the hospital scenes are happening here and now. The rest is Kate's memory of past events. These memory and dream sequences are amped up, pitched to a heightened, stylized quality through lights, costume, and sound.

ON THE REPETITION OF DIALOGUE

The four hospital scenes begin with repetition of some of the dialogue we heard in the prior hospital scene. This is done purposely and should be treated with conscious direction. In each ensuing repetition, a few words change. But the real change happens in the acting. Emotionality and intensity increase. If the play succeeds, the audience experiences the same language differently when it is repeated.

ON SILENCES

When the script calls for a silence, take the silence; really take it, don't hurry it, let it become real and part of the action.

Having directed two productions of CARNIVAL ROUND THE CENTRAL FIGURE in New York City, I am thrilled that this mysteriously potent play is being published, so that more directors and casts will have the unforgettable experience of living in its world, and sharing this very human and powerful story with their audiences.

CARNIVAL made its way to me in sort of a mystical way in 1996, when I was searching for a play to direct with our second year acting students at the Atlantic Theater Company's New York University undergraduate acting studio. One night I had gone to see another play by Diana Amsterdam, and she happened to overhear me talking about my desperate play search at intermission. The next morning a Fed Ex envelope was on my doorstep. Reading CARNIVAL on the way to school, the day I would have to turn in my decision, I was immediately captivated by this beautiful, gut-wrenching, human, and often hilarious work. Our students got to work on a new play—a rare and unusual circumstance for a group of 16 college students, mostly women. It felt like the play was written just for them. Our space was also special: because of a scheduling anomaly in the Atlantic season, we happened to have the 175 seat Atlantic theater to ourselves for the production (in those days, student productions were usually performed on top of a mainstage set).

This play electrified our cast, crew, and everyone who saw it. Its intense energy seemed to be the cause of a series of unexplainable coincidences, including an obituary for a man named identically to the actor Liam O'Brien, who played the dying Central Figure, listed in *The New York Times* the day of opening night. CARNIVAL is an unflinching look at our denial of death, framed in a circus motif—designer Rick Gradone and I used Fellini's *The Clowns* as an inspirational jumping off point to create a colorful, macabre, heightened, yet often heartfelt surround of color and movement. The play was intense, and also unforgettable, as 15 years later we found ourselves doing CARNIVAL again with several of the same actors. The entire cast in 2011 was Atlantic alumni, with five of the original cast returning; Shane LeCocq (Preacher), Christine Rowan (Sheila), Livia Scott (MaryAnn), Cynthia Silver (Becky Tupper) reprised their roles. How many actors get to revisit a treasured role 15 years later—in this case when they are now age-appropriate to the characters they so vividly created in 1996? Original cast member Kori Rushton, artistic director of I R T Theater, also produced in addition to acting the part of the Nurse. Designers were Atlantic alum and designer Eric Southern (lights), and frequent Atlantic designers Walt Spangler (in collaboration with Jisun Kim and Melissa Shakun, set), and Katja Andreiev (costumes). Music director was the wonderful David James Boyd. The new cast featured Danni Simon (Kate), Ed Stelz (Richard), Ted Caine (Central Figure), David Michael Kirby (Mr. Tupper, Kate's Father), and the choir, played by Carla Briscoe, Janna Emig, Brandon Kyle Goodman, Stephanie Hsu, Raymond Hill, and Rebecca Schoffer.

Karen Kohlhaas

(Lights up)

*(*THE NURSE *takes her seat. She will watch over the action for the duration of the play. If the other characters are to be onstage all the time, they take their places.)*

(Lights down)

(Lights up)

*(*THE CENTRAL FIGURE *[CF]is in bed under a sheet.)*

*(*SHEILA *sits in a chair at the foot of* CF's *bed. She holds an oversized needle at some distance from a piece of mending. She is frozen in this pose for a long beat before the action starts.)*

*(*SHEILA *mends with large movements.)*

SHEILA: You were a hundred percent right. They do clean up much better. I barely have to run a mop over them. Sometimes I add a little Step Saver. But I really don't have to. Mother couldn't believe it. I told her it was your idea. I gave you full credit! And it was so smart not to get white! When I think now that we lived all those years with white kitchen tiles! Were we crazy? Of course, you said and said and said. Of course I wouldn't listen. What is that surface? What's it called? Well, it's not all nubbly. Why they want to make kitchen tiles all nubbly is something I will never know. I know. Because they think that way the dirt will be camouflaged. Huh! What they fail to understand is that there are still certain people who notice that every day, the number of nubblies strangely increases! Yes! Till there are thousands of nubblies! Only it's not nubblies! It's dirt! Yes! Dirt! Only by then the dirt is so ingrained you can't get it out! Remember all the toothbrushes we went through? Lucky thing Mother's Mah Jong crowd saved their toothbrushes, did you ever write Mrs. Roseverweiss that thank-you note? It doesn't matter. She moved to Florida. The important thing is that when you come home this time, you will never, never have to scrub the kitchen floor with a toothbrush ever again! Isn't that wonderful? Just barely moisten the mop and voila! Of course you have to add a little bit of Pine Sol. Which reminds me. Janet finally painted her living room. I stopped by Friday, the place is still covered with cat hairs, but Stanley very kindly offered to go over our taxes. Of course he doesn't do the job you do, nobody adds and subtracts like you, Paul. They give their best. I'm not sure I like the color, though, a kind of orange pink like the flesh of a rotting cantaloupe. I know! There is something besides white! But she could have done wallpaper, they can afford it. You know what she said? 'Wall paper is paper.' Have you ever thought of that? They have to live with the same thing we do, bump into a floorboard, pieces of cardboard fall to the floor. Well! Some day we'll get out of there. I do love the smell of fresh paint. But we mustn't complain. It smells nice here, too, just today they were disinfecting the elevator. Extra strength. Have to. All sorts of bodily juices must drip right onto the floor. Which reminds me. When you get home, you must look at the air conditioner in the girls' room, it's dripping dripping dripping right onto the floor, I had Ben in but you know what a clod he is of course, nobody fixes things like you, they just see you coming and they—

(Enter KATE and RICHARD. SHEILA jumps to her feet.)

(During the following, KATE will stare at CF, horrified at what she sees.)

SHEILA: Hello!

KATE:	SHEILA:
Hi Sheila.	Oh, hello, Kate!
Hello—	

RICHARD: Richard.

SHEILA: Yes yes yes of course Richard! All the way from somewhere I'm so sorry I can't remember exactly where do you have that beautiful home? Excuse me, my mind has snapped.

KATE: Rye.

SHEILA: Rye! Rye, of course, Paul's cousin Monroe the doctor lives there, too, right, Paul? He doesn't feel much like talking today. *(Confidentially)* His mother always compared him to his cousin Monroe, you know, *(Loud)* but I personally consider Monroe a total blob, but it's so very very kind of you to come visit again and on a Sunday, too, look, Paul, look who's here, Paul, Kate from the office and her husband—

RICHARD: Friend—

SHEILA: Friend friend that's right, some things just go in one and out the other, sivbrain, that's what Paul calls me, don't you, honey, well, he doesn't really, he's so kind, *(Confidentially)* how do you think he looks?

(Long silence. KATE is not sure what to say. SHEILA breaks the silence:)

SHEILA: Better?

KATE:	RICHARD:
He, he looks—	Yes, I think so.

SHEILA: Everybody who comes today just says he looks so much better, you see, he ate a half a banana today, yes, we did, didn't we, we ate a whole half a banana, and we kept it all down, didn't we? And wasn't it good? He doesn't feel much like talking

today. Yes, it was very, very good, and the whole thing
went down, and the whole thing stayed down, and it
was the bigger half, the bottom half, the top half just
sort of fell you know how they do when they're half
rotten you never know what you're going to get at the
supermarket these days, I must tell you I can't wait to
get Paul home, he is the world's best shopper, that's
what you are, Paul, the world's best shopper, actually,
these were a gift, I probably let them sit too long, you
know you can't let bananas sit, you can't let anything
sit, you can't even let people sit, I know when I sit I
tend to go soft myself, don't you? If somebody tried
to eat me I'd probably just fall apart. (*Embarrassed,
flustered*) The things that come out of my mouth these
days I don't know I really don't—

(*Long silence*)

(KATE *is staring at* CF.)

SHEILA: You think he looks better? Kate? (*Pause*)

SHEILA: How do you think he looks compared to last
time you were here?

KATE: I don't know if I'd say that he looks—

RICHARD: Better, she thinks he looks better.

SHEILA: Everybody says so, even my mother and she
is such a critic, she's the kind of person who if you
ask her is the glass half empty or half full she says it
isn't washed properly, poor Paul poor Paul but Paul
is never going to have to wash glasses by hand ever
again, never never never that's a solemn promise, we
are going to get a dishwasher (*Confidentially*) I don't
know how we're going to swing it but we will! We
will! Because we must have time for our art! Paul is
a great artist, did you know that, Kate, at work? oh,
he never mentions it, he was a member of the Art
Students League in college, he can draw horses that

are so realistic you can picture their big, fat hooves just stomping you, of course, he had to stop when the girls came along, you probably have a full time maid in that big house of yours in Rye, right, Kate?

KATE: *(Still looking at* CF*)* Excuse me?

RICHARD: Sheila was just asking if we have a maid.

KATE: A what?

RICHARD: No.

SHEILA: No? But you can afford it. Now that you got that big promotion at work you can afford it, right?

KATE: I'm sorry. I'm just—just stunned—he looks, so, differ—

RICHARD: *(Cutting off* KATE's *last word)* Kate feels that she couldn't stand to have somebody waiting on her.

SHEILA: Omigod isn't that nice! Isn't that thoughtful! Of course these people can use the work half of them are out on the street begging but isn't that nice! Paul, don't you wish you were married to somebody like that? He doesn't feel much like talking.

*(*SHEILA *turns and sees* KATE, *moving toward* CF.*)*

SHEILA: Kate, darling, where are you going? Please don't breathe on him. Throw him a kiss. Like I do. Here, Paul! Catch, Paul! Here, Paul! Catch, Paul! Here!

(Exit stage or to sidelines SHEILA, RICHARD *and* KATE.*)*

(Lights up on MARYANNE, *in an official looking dress.)*

(A pale light remains on CF, *who now lies still, eyes closed.)*

MARYANNE: Let us say, then, that there are fourteen patients in a ward for the terminally ill. Time passes. There are ten patients. Time passes. There are six patients. Time passes. There are three patients. Time passes. There is just one patient left. And that one patient, my friends, gets out of bed one morning, gets dressed, walks out of the hospital and resumes his life. *(Pause)* For five years, thanks to the generosity and the farsightedness of the people here at Memorial Grace, I have had the opportunity to study that one patient. The survivor. *(Pause)* Who is the survivor? What sets the survivor apart from the others who succumb to their seemingly inevitable fate?

(Lights up on a screen, a Powerpoint Presentation. MARYANNE may be controlling it with a remote, or it is controlled from another place; either way, she is commanding the Presentation.)

(The word STUPIDITY comes up on the screen.)

MARYANNE: Stupidity. That's right. The survivor is too stupid to believe that he is going to die.

(The word: STUBBORNESS on screen.)

MARYANNE: Stubbornness. That's right. The survivor is too stubborn to give in to the demands of the cancer or the virus or the bacteria.

(The word: CONCEIT on screen.)

MARYANNE: Conceit. That's right. The survivor believes he is too important to die. He cannot, in fact, imagine the world going on without him.

(The word: GREED on screen.)

MARYANNE: Greed. That's right. The survivor has not had his fill of life, he wants more, he insists on it, more, more more!

(The word: COMPETITIVENESS on screen.)

MARYANNE: Competitiveness. That's right. The survivor must prove that he is stronger than everybody else. Yes?

(Light on KATE in the audience.)

KATE: *(From the audience)* But—maybe I don't understand but—doesn't everybody die?

MARYANNE: I'm sorry, I don't think they can hear you in the back. Would you repeat that? Stand up, please.

KATE: *(Stands)* I said, I'm asking, doesn't everybody die?

MARYANNE: I'm glad you asked that. This lovely young woman asked, "Doesn't everybody die?" Statistically, yes. You may sit down, dear. But simply because something has always happened does not mean that it will always happen. If we stood with Adam and Eve at the beginning of time, and Adam dropped dead, there would still be a fifty percent chance that Eve would never die. True. Many, many have died since then. So far as we know, everyone has died. However. There is still one chance in nineteen-point-four billion of not dying. Well, my friends. If you play, you may not win. But if you don't play, you'll inevitably lose. I am here today to tell you that it is possible to be a survivor. Some day somebody will come along who is so stupid, so stubborn, so conceited, so greedy, and so competitive—

(A list of words: STUPID STUBBORN CONCEITED GREEDY COMPETITIVE *on screen.)*

MARYANNE: —that he—or she—will break the statistical noose. *(Picking out people in the audience)* Will it be you? Will it be you? Will it be this sweet young woman who asked the obvious question?

*(*THE NURSE, *carrying an oversized syringe, approaches* CF's *bed.)*

MARYANNE: Will it be you? Will it be you? You look like a self-confident person, will it be you?

(Overlapping, as lights fade on KATE *and* MARYANNE:)*

MARYANNE: *(Speaking to people in the audience)* Will it be you? You? You? You? You?

NURSE: *(Overlapping* MARYANNE'*s final questions, voice amplified)* Come on. Come on now. Come on. Come on now.

(Lights higher on the bed in the middle of the stage. During the following, NURSE *draws blood from* CF.*)*

NURSE: Now come on, baby. Give just a little to Mama. I know you're tired. I know you don't think you got another drop to give. But you just got to give one more drop to Mama. Just one more precious little drop. Cause we got to see how we are. Now. How we gonna see how we are if we don't give just one more drop? There's a good vein. There's a good vein. One more drop. *(With her syringe full of blood, she returns to her seat as…)*

*(*THE CHOIR *enter, one by one. They are singing* Amazing Grace, *slowly like a dirge.)*

*(Suddenly, with tremendous energy…*THE PREACHER *enters. He is hooked to a mic, and the presence of T V cameras becomes real or suggested.)*

(On the screen, a show title: SPEAK STRAIGHT TO JESUS.*)*

(During the following, CF *suffers a kind of spasm in which* CF *tosses jerkily from side to side.* CF *then folds up, spent, into a fetal position.)*

PREACHER: One. Two. Glory Hallelu!

(The singing of Amazing Grace *goes up-tempo and upbeat, with great energy and excitement.* THE PREACHER *shakes hands with the audience.)*

PREACHER: *(To the audience)* Good mornin', Good mornin', welcome, welcome to Speak Straight to Jesus, how are you today… *(Etcetera, ad lib as needed)*

(THE PREACHER *dances with his Choir; they sing and dance.
Finally, he dances to his place on the dais, below the sign
that says* SPEAK STRAIGHT TO JESUS. *He is electric
with energy.*)

PREACHER: Thank you thank you, yes, thank you,
thank you Lord. *(Opens his Bible)* And now. Let us
read from the Holy Scriptures. From the 30th chapter
of Deuteronomy, Verse 16 through 19, we read: "I
command thee this day to love the Lord thy God, to
walk in His ways, and to keep His commandments and
His statutes and His ordinances; then thou shalt live
and multiply. But if thy heart turn away, and thou wilt
not hear, but shalt be drawn away, I declare unto you
this day, that ye shall surely perish. I call heaven and
earth to witness against you this day, that I have set
before thee life and death, the blessing and the curse;
therefore choose life." Amen. *(Closes Bible)*

THE CHOIR: *(Singing)* Amen! Amen! Amennnnnn!

(THE PREACHER *walks dramatically the length of the stage,
looking at the audience.*)

PREACHER: What do we find here? "I have set before
thee life and death, the blessing and the curse;
therefore choose life." Life. And death. The blessing.
And the curse. Brothers and sisters. In fifteen years
broadcasting the Gospel into your living rooms over
the holy airwaves of Speak Straight to Jesus, I have
never, I say never, been so moved by the Spirit as I am
today, as it manifests in these divinely inspired words:
Life. The blessing. Death. The curse. What is God
telling us? *(Pause)* Every single one of us in this room
has smelled coffee in the morning and looked into the
eyes of a child and used his hands to do some good
work and swam and eaten and drank and laughed
and played ball and kissed our beautiful wives, every
single one of us has been gifted heavenly gifted with

the blessing. Life. But the problematic part and I say problematic only because our minds in the sight of the greatness of the Lord are so limited, the problematic part is the curse. Death. Now we are all Christians here. We know that Death is not the curse, we know this because the holy scriptures tell us this, the holy scriptures tell us over and over that those who accept Jesus Christ shall be exalted forever into the kingdom of heaven and enjoy Life Everlasting, so how can death be the curse? But can the holy scriptures contain a contradiction?

THE CHOIR: *(Singing, one by one)*

NO

NO

NO

NO

NO

NO

PREACHER: Therefore it is incumbent upon us, brothers and sisters, to discover the weakness in our own minds that perceives a contradiction and I tell you that I have studied this verse long and hard and prayed for inspiration, and I tell you that the answer is here with us. This morning. Please welcome our guests on Speak Straight to Jesus, John and Becky Tupper.

(Dramatic organ music)

(Enter JOHN and BECKY.)

(CF grasps the handlebars of the bed and with an extraordinary effort pulls up, staring into space.

CF: Ayahayahayahayahayahayahayahayahayah

(JOHN and BECKY stand, heads bowed. CF's unearthly wailing overlaps the following for a beat, then fades:)

PREACHER: (*Speaking directly into the camera*) Jim, stop eating those eggs 'n' bacon. Martha, stop sweeping up those crumbs. Heather, stop fussing over what you're going to wear to church and Billy, stop bouncing that ball. And look at them. Just look at them.

(*Long beat, while the camera plays over* JOHN *and* BECKY)

PREACHER: And listen. To the story of John and Becky Tupper of Drayton Plains, Michigan. One week ago they were lost. And now they're saved.

(*Dramatic organ music*)

(*The light grows on* JOHN *and* BECKY. *It grows and grows until it is an intense spotlight. All else is blackness except CF, grasping the handlebars, sitting up in bed in the pale, pale light.*)

THE CHOIR: (*A hymn sung in an upbeat fashion, all smiles*)
The way to Jesus is not always easy.
The way to Jesus is fraught with pain.
Heartbreak undoes the latch to Jesus.
And grief uncovers the greatest gain.

(*CF collapses, spent.*)

PREACHER: John and Becky Tupper. Speak Straight To Jesus!

(THE PREACHER *exits, leaving* JOHN *and* BECKY *in the hot spotlight.*)

(*A too-long silence.*)

JOHN: We had a—have a daughter. A beautiful daughter. She's all of sixteen. She—

(BECKY *begins to cry softly.*)

JOHN: My wife. We had a daughter. A beautiful daughter. She's all of sixteen. Now she's in the hospital.

(During the following, THE CHOIR *will continue to sing, all smiles,* The Way to Jesus *in very soft, hushpuppy voices.)*

JOHN: She's. She's. Our daughter. Her name is Pamela. She's all of sixteen. Now she's in the hospital. She's dying. Our daughter Pamela is dying.

(The mother, BECKY, *bursts into tears. The sound of* BECKY's *weeping rises till it fills the theater, becoming uncomfortable.)*

(Exit JOHN *and* BECKY. *Lights fade. All sounds out)*

(Lights up on CF *with* SHEILA, RICHARD *and* KATE.)

SHEILA: How do you think he looks compared to last time you were here?

KATE: I don't know if I'd say that he looks—

RICHARD: Better, she thinks he looks better.

SHEILA: Everybody says so, even my mother and she is such a critic, she's the kind of person who if you ask her is the glass half empty or half full she says it's filthy, poor Paul poor Paul but Paul is never going to have to wash glasses by hand ever again, never never never that's a solemn promise, we are going to get a dishwasher *(Confidentially)* I don't know how we're going to swing it but we will! We will! Because we must have time for our art! Paul is a great artist, did you know that, Kate? He wanted to be a painter but of course you can't raise two children on that, can you, he used to teach at the Art Students League did you know? He can draw horses that are so realistic you can picture their big, fat hooves just stomping you, now he never picks up a brush at all, says it hurts him, isn't that silly, I say paint, paint, you probably have a full time maid in that big house of yours in Rye, right, Kate?

KATE: *(Still staring at* CF*)* Excuse me?

(During the following, KATE *will walk toward* CF *as if she's inexorably drawn to him.)*

RICHARD: Sheila was just asking if we have a maid.

KATE: A what?

RICHARD: No.

SHEILA: No? But you can afford it. Now that you got that big promotion at work boy didn't that come as a surprise to everyone, you can afford it, right?

KATE: I'm sorry. I'm just I'm just—shocked, seeing him this—wasted, this—destr

RICHARD: *(Cutting off her last word)* Kate feels that she couldn't stand to have somebody waiting on her.

SHEILA: Omigod isn't that nice! Isn't that thoughtful! Of course these people can use the work half of them are out on the street begging but isn't that nice! Kate, darling, what are you doing? Please don't breathe on him. Throw him a kiss. Like I do. Here, Paul! Catch, Paul! Kate, please! Don't breathe on him. He's just a welcome mat for every germ in the world.

KATE: Don't you think, isn't it better for him to have someone close than to worry about germs now, can't you see that he's—

RICHARD: Hup! Sheila, I'm sorry but we really have to go. My mother's expecting us for dinner. Pot roast.

SHEILA: Go? But of course you're not going to go. You just got here. Everybody just comes in and says two words and runs off I never saw such busy, go? Stay. I'm just saying that Kate should be careful not to breathe on him.

RICHARD: We have to go.

KATE: I want to stay.

RICHARD: We need to head out now!

KATE: I want to talk to him.

SHEILA: Talk to him? Oh no, I don't think that's such a good idea, he's very tired and he doesn't really feel much like talking today, that's why I have his TV on.

KATE: And is that, is that good for him right now? do you think he wants that blue light on his face, if he doesn't he can't ask to turn it off, I mean he's, he's obviously—

RICHARD: Okay! Okay! We'll stay! Let's sit down and we'll stay, now, Kate, okay! Sit down. KATE! Sit. Sh.

(KATE *sits. They all sit. Silence. The silence lasts and lasts while* SHEILA *searches for a way to fill it. Finally:*)

SHEILA: So your mother makes pot roast?

RICHARD: Yes.

SHEILA: What kind of pot roast? brisket or round?

RICHARD: Meat.

SHEILA: Meat! Aren't men cute?

(*During the following,* SHEILA, *defending against* KATE's *gaze, gets up and neatens CF: wipes his mouth, adjusts his hospital gown, etc.*)

SHEILA: When I first got Paul, he thought that to fry an egg you put it in the pan with the shell on! But now you know what? He does most of the cooking! Don't you, Paul? See? He just doesn't feel much like talking. (*Directly to* KATE) That's why I have his T V on. Pineapple chicken. Beef bourgignon. Linguini with white clam sauce although of course we don't use real clams, the girls are so allergic, I bet you can afford to eat in the best restaurants, what are you staring at, Kate?

RICHARD: I'm sorry, we really better go.

SHEILA: Go? No! Don't go! Stay. I don't mind if Kate wants to look at Paul, everybody looks at Paul, after all, there's no denying, he has changed quite a lot! But he looks so much better today! He's just tired. *(To* KATE*)* That's why I have his T V on.

RICHARD: We better go.

SHEILA: No! Wait! Do you want to see something disgusting? You won't believe this. I keep it at the nurse's station for safekeeping, I'll be right back! *(Pops out, pops in)* You won't let him leave, will you, Kate? Pot roast only gets better. *(Pops out, pops in)* You won't leave, will you?

KATE: I'm not going anywhere.

(SHEILA exits.)

RICHARD: What do you mean, you're not going anywhere? We're leaving.

KATE: She has the television on.

RICHARD: We'll just wait for her to come back, then we'll say good-night, and we're out of here.

KATE: She has the window closed. He can't breathe.

RICHARD: That's not your business.

KATE: Open the windows. Turn off the T V. He's—

KATE:	RICHARD:
—dying, Richard.	Shhhhhh
He is, he's —	Shh

RICHARD: We don't know that.

KATE: Yes. We do know it. We can see it. He's hardly even here, he's—

RICHARD: Shh we don't know he's anythinging, we're not doctors.

KATE: He looks exactly like Pamela looked.

RICHARD: Pamela? That was ten years ago.

KATE: Yes, and she looked like this. And she died. And nobody ever said it to her. Paul wants someone to say (*lovingly, but not to Paul*) Paul, you're dying.

RICHARD: Why would he want that?

KATE: Because he knows. And if nobody says anything, it's like, he's all alone.

RICHARD: I doubt he knows he's alone, he's hardly even here, he doesn't know anything.

KATE: He knows he's dying. Of course he does.

RICHARD: Okay. Maybe. (*Beat*) But not you.

KATE: Why not me?

RICHARD: You can't get this close to this, you already have bad dreams. Let somebody else do it: his wife, his doctor—

KATE:	RICHARD:
But they're not.	but not you.

RICHARD: Come on, we're getting out of here.

(RICHARD *takes* KATE *by the arm but she pulls away.*)

(KATE *approaches* CF.)

KATE: (*Going closer to* CF) Paul? Paul?

KATE:	RICHARD:
Paul?	Kate.
Paul, hello.	Come on.

RICHARD: Kate. Kate! For God's sake, don't touch him!

Freeze RICHARD and KATE.

(CF *goes into a kind of spasm, which continues for a time.*)

CF: Ayahayahayahayahayahayahayahayahayah

(*As the sound of* CF's *unearthly wailing fades*)

(*Lights down on* RICHARD *and* KATE.)

(Lights gradually rise on THE CHOIR, *who are kneeling and silently praying, with much concentration.)*

(A pale light remains on CF who nows lies still, eyes closed.)

CHOIR MEMBER: *(Praying)* I am not going to die.

CHOIR MEMBER: *(Praying)* I am not going to die.

CHOIR MEMBER: *(Praying)* I am not going to die.

(Repeat as necessary. The CHOIR MEMBERS *grow increasingly jubilant as they say these words.)*

(They scuttle about on their knees, taking various jubilant positions, as they start "receiving"...)

(Overlapping:)

CHOIR MEMBER: The Lord will save me I will not die!

CHOIR MEMBER: The Lord will save me I will not die!

CHOIR MEMBER: The Lord will save me I will not die!

(They are receiving the grace of the Lord like bullets hitting their balletic, acrobatic bodies.)

(Building into a frenzy of receiving the Grace:)

ENTIRE CHOIR: *(Mixed up, pieces of language grabbed)* I will not will not will not will not the Lord is in me the Lord is saving me the Lord is shielding me the Lord will keep me the Lord will save me I will not I will not I will not die I will never die I don't have to die I am saved I am saved I do not die I do not die I do not die I do not die

(The word "die" transforms into the sound of a chorus of angels singing a single high, clear note, begins and grows and mingles with the CHOIR, *takes over, and then abruptly stops.)*

(In the distance, there is the sound of a woman, weeping.)

(Lights up on the screen. A slide of a chubby baby, sitting in a playpen in a backyard.)

(An intense spotlight on JOHN *and* BECKY. BECKY *is the woman, weeping. All else is blackness except* CF *in the pale, pale light.)*

JOHN: *(Trying to comfort* BECKY*)* My wife. My wife. Excuse me.

(Enter THE PREACHER.*)*

PREACHER: Heartbreak undoes the latch to Jesus.

THE CHOIR: Heartbreak undoes the latch to Jesus!

BECKY: Go on. I'm all right. Go on.

JOHN: And that was the last time.

PREACHER: Tell me, John. Put your arm around her, it's all right. Tell me, John. During this period, did you suspect that your daughter was abusing alcohol?

JOHN: No, Bob, we didn't.

PREACHER: Did you suspect that she was engaging in lustful fornication?

BECKY: No!

JOHN: No, Bob, we didn't.

PREACHER: Were you and Becky going to Church at this time?

JOHN: No. No, we were not going to Church at this time, Bob.

PREACHER: *(Meaningfully, into the camera)* Heartbreak undoes the latch to Jesus. Amen.

THE CHOIR: *(Singing)* Amen. Amen. Amennnnn.

PREACHER: Amen.

JOHN: Amen.

PREACHER: And now. I want to talk a moment with Becky.

You know. Mothers are special. We all remember how we felt when we crawled up in the lap of our mother, and she put her arms around us and made us feel that everything was all right. And from her good lips we first learned to say, Praise The Lord.

THE CHOIR: Praise The Lord.

PREACHER: Praise The Lord.

THE CHOIR: Praise the Lord Praise the Lord Praise the Praise the Praise the Lord Lord Praise the Lord the Lord

(THE CHOIR *exclaims into a frenzy that* THE PREACHER *abruptly cuts off with a snap of fingers or wave of hand:)*

PREACHER: YES! Praise The Lord. In a way, mothers are like Jesus. Because mothers would take unto themselves the pain of their children to spare their children pain. Do you know what I'm talking about, Becky?

BECKY: Yes.

PREACHER: I know you do. Now Becky. You have a daughter. Sixteen year old Pamela. Pamela is sick unto death. Is that right?

BECKY: Yes.

PREACHER: Now I am going to ask you to do something for me, Becky. And it won't be easy. But if you can do this for me, the Lord will ease your terrible pain. Now, Becky. Forget the studio audience. Forget the T V cameras. Forget the nine million viewers watching you from coast to coast and in Europe, South America, Russia and even ungodly China.

(*A bright hot spotlight on* BECKY. *The slide of the chubby baby is also illuminated. All else—except* CF *in the pale light—fades into blackness.*)

(*We continue to hear* THE PREACHER's *voice.*)

PREACHER: You are standing on the hilltop of your soul. Standing face to face with Jesus. Becky Tupper. SPEAK STRAIGHT TO JESUS!

(*Exit* THE PREACHER. *Silence*)

(BECKY *stares, eyes squinting, into the spotlight.*)

BECKY: I—John—Where are you? John? Are you here? (*Silence*) Are you here, John? I—John? Excuse me. John?

(*The slide changes. From a chubby baby, to a toddler snapping her underpants, to a little girl holding a doll, to a pre-teenager posing on a tabletop, to a teenage girl. A beautiful teenage girl. Walking down a country road. To a beautiful teenage girl, walking down a country road with* KATE. *To* CF. *CF in a hospital bed. CF's face. Closer on CF's face.*)

BECKY: Jesus! Punish me! It was my fault, Jesus! My fault! Don't punish her! Punish me! I turned away! I would not hear! Save her! I beg you, Jesus! It was my fault! All my fault! Let me take it, Jesus! I beg you! Give it to me! I deserve it! I want it! Jesus! Punish me!

(*Blackout*)

(*Silence*)

(*A very pale light remains on* CF.)

(*Enter* THE NURSE *with her giant syringe.*)

(*She spends time putting a cuff on* CF's *arm and feeling for a vein.*)

(*During the following, dramatic organ music rises.*)

NURSE: (*Crooning maternally/seductively, voice amplified*) Come on, sweetie, come on. Just give a little bit more to Mama. Cause we know you got one more drop. And we got to have one more drop. Come on baby. Hard as it is. All right. All right. There's a good vein. There's a good vein. (*She exits with her giant syringe, now filled with very red blood.*)

(The dramatic organ music crescendos.)

ANNOUNCER'S VOICE: *(O S)* And now...back to
...SPEEEEEAAK STRAIGHT TO: JESUS!

PREACHER: Thank you, F J. We're here today coming to
you live from Okokee Michigan in the great heartland
of the U! S! A! With John & Becky Tupper, who have
taken the hard road to Jesus. Now for all of you who
may have missed Becky's heartrending plea to the
Lord, can we see that one more time, F J?

ANNOUNCER: Sure, Bob.

(Replay video:)

BECKY: *(On screen)* Jesus! Punish me! It was my fault,
Jesus! My fault! Don't punish her! Punish me! I turned
away! I would not hear! Save her! I beg you, Jesus! It
was my fault! All my fault! Let me take it, Jesus! I beg
you! Give it to me! I deserve it! I want it! Jesus! Punish
me!

PREACHER: And now... Here they are... This week's
Speakers to Jesus... John and Becky Tupper!

*(Lights up on JOHN and BECKY, tan, decked-out, and
glowing with good health and prosperity.)*

*(They walk up to THE PREACHER, who holds the mic to
them.)*

PREACHER: You feel better now, Becky?

BECKY: Yes I do.

PREACHER: I know you do. And I know Jesus is
listening.

And how about you, John? Do you feel better?

JOHN: Yes I do, Bob.

PREACHER: Well that's good. Because the hard road to
Jesus is not fully traversed just yet. Are you girded by
the Lord, Becky?

BECKY: Yes I am, Bob.

PREACHER: Are you girded by the Lord, John?

JOHN: Praise the Lord, Bob.

PREACHER: Good. Now let's see that last slide of Pamela Tupper one more time.

(CF *struggles up in bed.*)

(CF *in bed is* CF *on the screen.*)

CF: Ayahayahayahayahayahayahayahayahayah

(BECKY *hides her face in* JOHN's *chest, then forces herself to look at* CF *on the screen. Her quiet sobbing punctuates the following:*)

PREACHER: *(Referring to the screen)* Do you believe it? Do you believe that this, this *thing* was, just a few short years ago, a virginal teenage girl? We must ask ourselves, the Lord wants us to ask ourselves, how, WHY, does the Lord take a beautiful young girl, a girl who only a few short years ago was virginal and pure and untouched, a girl who walked by the wayside by the fields of flowers in her good town of Drayton Plains, Michigan, and turn her into this. This. A monster.

(CF *falls back, exhausted.*)

PREACHER: The beauty. Turns into. The beast.

CHOIR: The beauty.

PREACHER: The beauty, Lord, turns into.

CHOIR: Turns into.

PREACHER: The beast.

(THE PREACHER *maintains a long silence, turning his back to the audience. When he turns again, his voice and demeanor have changed. He is now the angel of retribution. During the following,* JOHN *will hold* BECKY *very tight but they will force themselves to listen.*)

PREACHER: *(Like a madman)* WHY? WHY, YOU ASK! I'll tell you why. "I call Heaven and Earth to witness against you this day, that I have set before thee life and death, therefore choose life." *Choose* life. *Choose* life. How do we choose life? Do we know how to choose life? Are we taught how to choose life? Perhaps we remember, perhaps one or two of us may remember that the Lord gave us Ten rules. Did he call these ten rules the Ten Suggestions? Did he call these ten rules the Ten Requests? Did he call these ten rules the Ten Directives? What did he call them?

CHOIR MEMBER: The Ten Commandments.

PREACHER: What?

CHOIR MEMBER: The Ten Commandments.

PREACHER: What?

CHOIR MEMBER: The Ten Commandments.

PREACHER: What? I can't hear you!

CHOIR MEMBER: The Ten Commandments.

PREACHER: What? Louder!

CHOIR MEMBER: The Ten Commandments.

PREACHER: Say it again!

CHOIR MEMBER: The Ten Commandments.

PREACHER: Again!

CHOIR MEMBER: The Ten Commandments.

PREACHER: Again!

ENTIRE CHOIR: The Ten Commandments.

PREACHER: Say it in the audience!

CHOIR: The Ten Commandments.

PREACHER: Say it in Louisiana!

CHOIR: The Ten Commandments.

PREACHER: Say it in Alaska!

CHOIR: The Ten Commandments.

PREACHER: Say it in Rhode Island!

CHOIR: The Ten Commandments.

PREACHER: Commandments!

CHOIR: Commandments.

PREACHER: Commandments!

CHOIR: Commandments.

(Etcetera as the spirit builds into a frenzy.)

PREACHER: I have set before thee life! and death! the blessing! and the curse! Do you see it? Do you see the curse? Do you see the filth? *(Pointing to CF on the screen)* This child is not innocent! This child broke the Lord's Commandments! Defied His rules! Defiled her body! Sunk into the slime that Satan holds forth in the guise of pleasure and lust and sensual gratification, and now she is the slime. She is the slime. There is no shelter! There is no respite!

(During the following, PREACHER lays hands on the CHOIR, who scream and writhe in hellfire agony.)

PREACHER: The Lord will strike you right inside your mouth, right inside your ears, right inside your bowels, right inside your eyes, right inside your guts with the black filth slime curse that you have chosen!

CHOIR: Amen.

PREACHER: That you have chosen!

CHOIR: Amen.

PREACHER: *(Exhausted, sweaty, consumed)* That you have chosen, that you have chosen, that you have chosen. Therefore choose life!

CHOIR: Choose life!

PREACHER: Choose life!

CHOIR: Choose life!

PREACHER: Choose life!

CHOIR: Choose life!

PREACHER: *(Spent, falls to his knees)* LIFE

ANNOUNCER: Cut! That's a wrap, folks.

(Studio lights up; the T V taping is over.)

PREACHER: You got that? Good.

(Exit THE CHOIR *and* THE PREACHER, *and* JOHN *and* BECKY.*)*

*(*THE FOUR PEOPLE *enter with gauze or masks over their heads, and circle* CF's *bed.)*

PERSON ONE: So your mother makes pot roast.

PERSON TWO: Yes, she does.

PERSON THREE: What kind?

PERSON FOUR: Brisket or round?

PERSON ONE: Round.

PERSON TWO: I'm almost out of stockings.

PERSON THREE: Every single one has a run.

PERSON FOUR: Every single color has a run.

PERSON ONE: Black.

PERSON TWO: Grey.

PERSON THREE: White.

PERSON FOUR: Brown.

PERSON ONE: Pink.

PERSON TWO: How's the van?

PERSON THREE: Much better.

PERSON FOUR: Was it the transmission?

PERSON ONE: Just the clutch.

PERSON TWO: Lucky for you.

PERSON THREE: We got new kitchen tiles.

PERSON FOUR: They were so easy to install.

PERSON ONE: You simply peel off the back.

PERSON TWO: You can cut them with anything.

PERSON THREE: Scissors, knife.

PERSON FOUR: Forty minutes to get here.

PERSON ONE: Backed up over the bridge.

PERSON TWO: Ever take the tunnel?

PERSON THREE: I occasionally take the tunnel.

PERSON FOUR: I occasionally take the tunnel.

PERSON ONE: I occasionally take the tunnel.

PERSON TWO: I occasionally take the tunnel.

PERSON ONE: I do shop online sometimes.

PERSON TWO: Shipping is cheap.

PERSON THREE: Returns are simple.

PERSON FOUR: They make it easy.

(CF *brief silence*)

PERSON THREE: I hope I don't get a shut-off.

PERSON FOUR: Were you late paying your bill?

PERSON ONE: You know how that happens.

PERSON TWO: The envelope falls to the floor.

PERSON THREE: Or in the trash.

PERSON FOUR: Or the dog eats it.

PERSON ONE: Pay with your card.

PERSON TWO: You can always pay that way.

(*Enter* KATE.)

PERSON THREE: We never use real clams.

PERSON FOUR: Is there a substitute?

PERSON ONE: Textured vegetable protein.

PERSON TWO: No fishy aftertaste.

PERSON THREE: My kitchen floor is dirty.

KATE: It's you, isn't it?

(KATE *rips the hood off* PERSON THREE, *revealing* SHEILA.)

SHEILA: What are you doing? Don't do that. Give me that.

KATE: Say it to him. You've got to say it to him. PAUL! Don't be afraid. Everybody goes through what you are going through, everybody

(KATE *and* SHEILA *struggle.*)

KATE:	SHEILA:
PAUL! PAUL!	NURSE! NURSE!
EVERYBODY DIES!	HELP! HELP ME!
PAUL, GO	THERE'S A CRAZY
LET YOURSELF GO	WOMAN IN HERE!

SHEILA: GET HER!

(THE FOUR PEOPLE *chase* KATE *around* CF's *bed, almost catching her, snipping at her skirts.* KATE *tries to fend them off.*)

(*Enter* THE NURSE *with her giant syringe.*)

(*Overlapping:*)

PERSON ONE: It's her! Yes, it's her!

PERSON TWO: It's her! It's her!

ALL THE PERSONS: It's her, it's her, it's her, her her!

(THE NURSE, *holding her giant syringe, stands and stares at* KATE.)

KATE: Somebody has to comfort him. Please.

THE NURSE: I could stab you with this. It has the disease all over it.

(THE NURSE, *holding her giant syringe, continues to stare at* KATE.)

THE NURSE: *(Cheerily)* But. Visiting hours are almost over.

(*Abrupt blackout*)

(*If the director chooses to have an intermission, it happens here.*)

(*Lights up.*)

(*A bright light on* MARYANNE.)

MARYANNE: I am not particularly worried about global warming. I am a firm believer that every woman has the right to an abortion. I am a vegetarian. I am young. I am a libertarian. I am a lazy son of a bitch. I am an accountant. I am an artist. I am a Christian. I am a Muslim. I am a dreamer. I am a husband. I am a child. I am.

These two words and your faith in them are the great fortress that stands between you and Death.

We sit in our chairs. Cloaked and wrapped and defined in our personal I am's. We cannot begin to imagine the agony of the dying person. And this is how it should be. We are meant to live in the belly of a profound complacency. But the dying person? he or she is stripped of every defense. In the course of the diagnosis, the hospitalization, the drugs, the pity and the pain, the dying person suffers the loss of each and every I am till only one remains. I am alive. And then, that too dissolves, like a teardrop in the ocean. Except for the survivor! The survivor either from stupidity or the most profound courage refuses to give up his last remaining I am. I am alive. He clings to it, he cherishes it, he re-creates it second by second from the sheer exertion of his will, he—

KATE: *(Interrupting, from the audience)* But doesn't everybody die?

MARYANNE: Young lady, I have answered that question—

KATE: But you keep talking about The Survivor, but isn't that false hope?

MARYANNE: No hope is false. Let me put that in the positive. All hope is true.

KATE: Not if it's a lie.

MARYANNE: What is your name?

KATE: Kate.

MARYANNE: Kate what?

KATE: Kate Bandell.

MARYANNE: Kate Bandell, didn't anybody ever tell you that heckling is not polite? You have the right to your opinion but you do not have the right to come to my lectures and ask the same question over and over and over.

(Exit MARYANNE. THE PREACHER *enters with* THE CHOIR *who stand around the bed, hiding* CF.*)*

KATE: But it's really a very simple thing! *(Turns to audience)* Isn't it a very simple thing? Don't we all die? Answer me.

SHILL: *(Or actual audience member)* Yes.

KATE: Thank you.

PREACHER: Young lady. You can come in now.

(During the following, KATE *will appear much younger. Her bearing and demeanor are those of a teenage girl.)*

(KATE *blows a giant bubble gum bubble, and smartly pops it.*)

KATE: Make me.

PREACHER: Come on, Kate. Make it easy for yourself.

KATE: For me? That's a laugh. For you, you mean. Make it easy for you. Where's my father?

PREACHER: You'll have to come eventually.

KATE: I don't have to do anything, preacherman. You're probably fucking young boys—

(THE CHOIR *gasps and reels in unison.*)

KATE: Or sleeping with your big-titty secretary because you're really sick of your wife! (*Dripping with sarcasm*) Come on, admit it, make it easy for yourself. Where's my father?

PREACHER: He's not coming.

KATE: Bullshit!

(THE CHOIR *draws in its breath in horror at the word* KATE *has used.*)

KATE: (*Trying it again*) Bullshit!

(THE CHOIR *draws in its breath, reels and gasps.*)

KATE: Bullshit! Bullshit, bullshit, bullshit.

(*Much drawing-in of breath, reeling and gasping*)

KATE: Trained supertrained trained fuckin monkeys.

(THE CHOIR *draws in its breath.* KATE *laughs.*)

KATE: Y'know, they're funny, they really are.

PREACHER: They are high on The Lord.

KATE: My ass.

(THE CHOIR *draws in its breath and reels in unison. During the following, unseen by* KATE, MRS TUPPER *enters and stands at the head of the bed.*)

KATE: *(To* THE CHOIR*)* Watch out, don't faint, they'll have to take you to the hospital. *(Laughs)* That's a joke. When did you say my father is getting here?

PREACHER: Your father is not coming.

KATE: Play that game.

PREACHER: Your mother has prevailed, Kate.

KATE: That I can believe. But my father will be here. He's Jewish, you know.

PREACHER: We know.

KATE: Me and him personally slung your stupid Jesus up on the cross.

*(*THE CHOIR *gasps in horror and reels in unison.* KATE *laughs.)*

KATE: That's right! We personally slung your stupid Jesus up on the cross! And I'm not coming anywhere near you! I don't care what my mother says! I've seen you on T V! I've seen what you do! You try to make people into angels! Stupid, empty, clean airhead angels! Well, people are not kitchen floors! People can't be scrubbed like—

*(*THE PREACHER *makes a sign. Like the Red Sea,* THE CHOIR *parts, revealing CF.)*

KATE: …kitchen floors— Who's that?

PREACHER: This is your friend. Pamela.

KATE: I'm saying: Who's that old man?

PREACHER: This is your friend. Pamela.

KATE: My friend Pamela's in a hospital in Detroit. The Henry Ford Hospital. Named after the jerk who invented exhaust. I write her there every day.

PREACHER: Has she ever answered? *(Holds up CF's hand)* A gold ring with a heart. I believe you gave this to her.

KATE: That's not the same ring.

PREACHER: Come. See for yourself.

KATE: No. (*She sees* BECKY.) Mrs Tupper? What are you doing here?
Who's this old man in the bed? Mrs Tupper? What are you doing here? (*Realizing, screams*) MRS TUPPER.

(*The scream "MRS. TUPPERRRRRRRRRR" echoes.*)

(*Exit* THE CHOIR, THE PREACHER, *and* KATE. *A bright light remains on* CF, *who repeatedly sucks thumb and gags.*)

(*Lights up on* THE FOUR PEOPLE, *in a circle around* MARYANNE.)

MARYANNE: (*To* THE FOUR PEOPLE) Do not let her anywhere near the patients. She is determined to inform one of them that he is dying, I don't know which one, but I fear it may be your husband. She does not understand the power of the spoken word. She will kill him, sure as if she carried a knife. What is that sound?

(*Silence*)

MARYANNE: I thought I heard something. It sounded like sex. But that's impossible here. Quick! Look for her. And when you find her, bring her to me.

(THE FOUR PEOPLE *disperse to all corners, as if looking for someone. They search stealthily, like demon cats, into all corners.*)

(*Amazing Grace rises, sung by a single voice, very bluesy.*)

(THE NURSE *sings* Amazing Grace. THE NURSE *sits in a rocking chair, rocking the giant syringe in her lap, like a baby. She sings* Amazing Grace *very slowly, with long beats between lines.*)

(*Somewhere during this long drawn-out singing that fills the space…*THE FOUR PEOPLE *disperse and exit.*)

THE NURSE: Amazing grace.
(Beat)
How sweet the sound.
(Beat)
That saved a wretch.
(Beat)
Like me.
(Beat)
I once was lost.
(Beat)
But now I'm found.
(Beat)
Was blind.
(Beat)
But now I see.

(The lights rise on SHEILA, RICHARD *and* KATE. KATE *is standing at the edge of the area directly around CF's bed, staring at* THE NURSE.*)*

THE NURSE: Me, I talk to the veins. That's what I do. Sometimes it works. And sometimes it don't. The patient hates the needle but then he becomes addicted to it, also. Yes. The closer he comes to death, the more he depends on that poke to let him know he is alive. *(She turns and looks at* KATE.*)* It has the disease all over it.

*(*KATE *joins* SHEILA *and* RICHARD, *and the action resumes.)*

RICHARD: We need to head out now.

SHEILA: No! Wait! Do you want to see something disgusting? You won't believe this. I keep it at the nurse's station for safekeeping, I'll be right back! *(Pops out, pops in)* You won't let him leave, will you, Kate? Pot roast only gets better. *(Pops out, pops in)* You won't leave, will you?

KATE: I'm not going anywhere.

(SHEILA *exits.*)

RICHARD: What do you mean, you're not going anywhere? We're leaving.

KATE: She has the television on.

RICHARD: We'll just wait for her to come back, then we'll say good-night, and we're out of here.

KATE: She has the window closed. He can't breathe.

RICHARD: That's not your business.

KATE: Open the window. Turn off the T V. He's dying, Richard. He's dying.

RICHARD: Shh. We don't know that.

KATE: Yes. Yes. We know it. We can see it. We can look at him and see that he is dying.

RICHARD: We don't know that he's dying.

KATE: We know.

RICHARD: We're not doctors.

KATE: I know. I know. He looks exactly like Pamela.

RICHARD: Pamela was what, ten years ago? it's time to let that go.

(*A long beat. Overlap the following dialogue:*)

KATE: I wish my father were here.

RICHARD: Chhhhghh

KATE: I wish my father would walk in here right now—

RICHARD: Your father, your father—

KATE: And say the truth, my father would say the truth—

RICHARD: (*Cuts through*) He's dying! Fine! But there's nothing you can do about it.

KATE: I can let him know that somebody understands what's happening to him. He's so alone.

RICHARD: Okay. Maybe. *(Beat)* But not you.

KATE: Why not me?

RICHARD: You can't get this close to this, you already have bad dreams. Let somebody else do it: his wife, his doctor—

KATE:	RICHARD:
But they're not.	but not you.

RICHARD: Come on, we're getting out of here.

(RICHARD takes KATE by the arm but she pulls away. She walks towards CF.)

KATE: Paul? Paul?

KATE:	RICHARD:
Paul?	Kate.
Paul, hello.	Come on.

RICHARD: Kate. Kate! Did you ever sleep with him?

KATE: What?

RICHARD: Why do you care so much about this guy from work?

KATE: I care because he's, he's terrified.

RICHARD: Come away from him, okay? please.

(KATE goes to RICHARD.)

RICHARD: Kate. I love it that you're this person who feels everything so deeply, you know that. But you can't always make things better.

KATE: I know that.

RICHARD: And I guess it bothers me that sometimes, you don't know where the line is between you and the rest of the world.

KATE: I don't even know that that means. I just want to take him in my arms.

RICHARD: Did you sleep with him?

(*A long beat of silence,* RICHARD *waiting for* KATE's *answer.*)

KATE: He used to give me pencils. He always kept some on his desk in this purple cup. His desk was such a mess. He had a zillion pictures of his daughters, he was crazy about them. At six sharp, he'd walk out, he had the worst posture. He looked so beaten down. Once in a while, I'd catch him though. Drawing something. Some incredible vista of mountain and bursting suns in the corner of a legal pad. One night we were alone in the elevator. I felt him looking at me. It wasn't like desire or anything it was more like: Wistfulness, like, remembering something he thought he could never have again. I just took his head in my hands and

RICHARD: I don't want to hear this.

KATE: You asked.

RICHARD: I asked if you slept with him, that's all I wanted, not a whole story. There's such a thing as too much truth—

KATE:	RICHARD:
O K you're right.	too much truth
You're right.	gets toxic, it
I know: I tend	turns into a tape
to do that:	that just plays
I say too much	and plays

(*Enter* SHEILA, *carrying a seltzer bottle.*)

SHEILA: Yoohoo I'm back! And you're still here, aren't you good? You wouldn't believe what I had to go through to get this, they'd taken it all the way to the Green Zone, can you imagine, the nerve of these people, they think everything belongs to them, they really do, I know what you're thinking, Paul, it's not their fault, it's the way they were raised, he's always so generous. How is he? Any change?

KATE: No.

SHEILA: Did he throw up that banana?

KATE: No.

SHEILA: No? Isn't that wonderful? We ate a whole half banana and we kept it all down. He doesn't feel much like talking today. That's why I have his T V on. Oh but I'm almost forgetting, and you with that pot roast to get to, here, look at this. You won't believe this. This is the most disgusting thing I've ever seen, you're a lawyer, right, um -

RICHARD: Richard.

SHEILA: Richard! Richard Richard Richard. Maybe you can tell me if I have a case, Richard Richard Richard. *(She tips the seltzer bottle from side to side.)* Come close, look, come on! Come on. Look!

RICHARD: We really have to go.

SHEILA: Go? You don't really have to go this minute, do you? Stay, please, just for one—

CF: Ayahay

SHEILA: See? Paul wants you to stay and look at this, really, you don't want to miss this, it's the most disgusting thing you've ever seen, and not only that but it could make us rich, don't you want to see what could make us rich in a seltzer bottle? I won't ask for any free legal advice, Richard—

RICHARD: That's not the point—

SHEILA: I know how you must feel, everyplace you go, everybody just picking your brain—

RICHARD: Really, I'd be happy to give you advice if we weren't in a hurry—

SHEILA: It must be so annoying, everybody thinking oh goody, here's a lawyer, pop all my legal questions-

RICHARD: *(An outburst)* It's got nothing to do with that! Okay? Now are we going? Kate?

(SHEILA *thrusts the bottle in front of* RICHARD'*s eyes, and tips it this way and that.*)

SHEILA: What do you see?

RICHARD: Nothing. Water. Seltzer. Kate?

SHEILA: And what else?

RICHARD: Bubbles, for God's sake it's a damn seltzer bottle.

SHEILA: But what else? Come on, Kate. Come on. You won't believe what's in here. Look, Richard. Don't you see them? Two baby cockroaches! And it's never been opened! Well? Do you see them?

RICHARD: Yes. I see them. There they are. Now let's go.

(SHEILA *holds out the seltzer bottle to* KATE.)

SHEILA: Well, let Kate see them, for goodness sake, let Kate have a look.

KATE: I'm sorry. I don't see anything.

SHEILA: Look.

KATE: I don't see anything in here.

SHEILA: Look at the little feet. Look at the little antennae.

KATE: I think that's just the way the light plays.

SHEILA: The light can't make cockroaches.

KATE: I don't see them.

SHEILA: Look! There goes one! There goes the other one!

KATE: I don't see them.

SHEILA: Well, everybody sees them. The nurses. Even the surgeon. I'm planning a class action suit against Canada Dry.

KATE: They're not there.

SHEILA: Of course they are. Right before your eyes.

KATE: My eyes don't see them.

SHEILA: It's not a question of your eyes.

KATE: My eyes are looking.

SHEILA: They're either there or they're not there.

KATE: Look at your husband, then.

RICHARD: Kate.

SHEILA: Excuse me?

KATE: I said Look at your husband.

RICHARD: Kate. Let's go. Now.

SHEILA: I'm sorry, you want me to look at my husband? I always look at my husband. Is this a little parlor game or something?

KATE: Look at your husband. What do you see?

SHEILA: Look at my husband. What do I see?

KATE: What do you see?

RICHARD: I'm going. I'm going now. Kate.

KATE: Okay. Go. Go, get out of here if you need to!

(*Exit* RICHARD.)

KATE: Look at your husband. And tell me the truth about what you see.

(*Enter* RICHARD.)

RICHARD: Come on. This isn't going to do anybody any good. Come on.

(RICHARD *tries to pull* KATE *out with him. She wrenches away.*)

(SHEILA *cowers away, terrified of* KATE.)

KATE: Say it. Go on, say it. You know the truth.

(*Enter* MARYANNE.)

SHEILA: Maryanne! Oh, Maryanne! Oh god thank god Maryanne! Yes, we have an appointment now, don't we? Five o'clock. Well, I was just saying, there was just somebody saying, my friend, really, a friend of Paul's, a co-worker and her husband, Kate and—Richard! Richard! They were just leaving.

MARYANNE: (*Seeing* KATE) You.

KATE: Hi, Maryanne.

SHEILA: Do you know each other?

MARYANNE: This is the young lady who comes to my lectures every week and she always disrupts with the same question.

KATE: It's a very simple question. Doesn't everybody die?

SHEILA: Excuse me?

MARYANNE: And how is he today, Sheila?

SHEILA: Much better! Much much better! He ate a whole half banana and he didn't puke!

MARYANNE: That's wonderful. How long has it been?

SHEILA: Three weeks. He just doesn't feel much like talking. That's why I have his T V on.

(MARYANNE *walks to* CF, *gazes at him like a scientist gazing at a beloved petri dish. She holds out her hands for the others to take, calmly and placidly. She speaks in clear ringing tones.)*

MARYANNE: Good evening, Paul. It's I, Maryanne. I'm the hospital psychologist and I come here every evening at five o'clock. You are Paul Glass. You are an accountant. You are thirty-eight years old. You are husband to Sheila. Father to Sondra and Beverly. You live at 37 Fieldstone Drive in Hartsdale, New York. You are in the hospital now. You are fighting the disease. And if you can summon the courage and the winning attitude, you, Paul, will soon go home.

CF: I.

(MARYANNE turns to SHEILA, KATE and RICHARD.)

(MARYANNE's face glows with triumph.)

(An abrupt blackout)

(In the total darkness, a sound is heard. A light rises on THE NURSE in the rocking chair, rocking the giant syringe like a baby.)

(The sound is like a woman in pain, at first. But as it grows, clearly, it is the sound of a woman having sex, getting louder.)

(Lights up on THE CHOIR. They are kneeling, praying, but taking tiny steps with their knees, as if repelled by something in their midst.)

(As they part, they reveal KATE. Repulsed, THE CHOIR inches further and further away from KATE till she is isolated. It becomes clear that KATE is making the sounds of sex.)

(An abrupt blackout. Silence)

(A pale light remains on CF, who lies now curled into a fetal position, moved only by an occasional tremor.)

(Lights up on THE CHOIR, scattered on their knees across the stage.)

(One by one, THE CHOIR *stands with a charismatic, acrobatic build of gospel fervor.)*

CHOIR MEMBER: I am.

CHOIR MEMBER: I am.

CHOIR MEMBER: I am.

CHOIR MEMBER: I am.

CHOIR MEMBER: I am!

CHOIR MEMBER: I am!

CHOIR MEMBER: I am!

CHOIR MEMBER: I am!

CHOIR MEMBER: I am!

ENTIRE CHOIR: *(Rejoicing)* I am! I am! I am! I AM AM AM AM AM AM AM AM AM AM AM AM AM AM AM

(It becomes apparent that the space where KATE *was kneeling is now empty. Enter* THE PREACHER.*)*

PREACHER: There were two little girls who lived in a little town right outside Detroit, Michigan, U S A. Two beautiful little girls.

(Slide of Pamela and KATE*)*

(During the following, successive slides of Pamela and KATE *in various teenage-girl activities.)*

PREACHER: Maybe just like your little girl, Jim. Just like your little girl, Andy. Just like your little girl, Bud. Just like your little girl, Jose. Just like your little girl, Hans. Just like your little girl, Abdul. Just like your little girl, Pierre. Just like your little girl, Chan. Just like your little girl. Just like my little girl. Bring your daughters to the television, now. Go on. Bring them. There is something they need to see.

(The slides of Pamela and KATE *continue. Then slides which go closer and closer on Pamela's lovely face.)*

PREACHER: *(Looking at the slides)* Yes sir. You watch your precious little girl blossom into a beautiful woman, full of promise and light. And you pray, as I know I have prayed, as I know every good father prays that his little girl will never be tempted by anything that can sully her God-given innocence. Then one day you find out your beautiful little girl has been having sex with every boy in the neighborhood.

(Lights up on KATE, *who kneels, head bowed.)*

PREACHER: Do you recognize this little girl? Do you know who she is?

(A slide of Pamela and KATE. *A closeup of* KATE*)*

PREACHER: Lift your head, Kate. Yes. That's right. This is the mystery girl we've been seeing right here on this show in these real life family slides of Pamela Tupper, the teenager who got trapped in Satan's Silky Web. This is Kate. Kate Bandell. I tracked her down. I forced her to listen to the truth and when I say forced I mean forced, because Satan injects his victims with a sweet poison that makes them defend him even as his fangs turn their flesh to excrement. But Jesus gave me the strength to rescue her from that hideous maw, and Lord be praised—

CHOIR: Lord be praised—

PREACHER: Amen—

CHOIR: Amen—

PREACHER: Amen! And so Kate is here with us today. Here to witness the truth to Jesus and the world. Tell us, Kate. How many boys did your friend Pamela have sex with?

KATE: Four.

PREACHER: Four different boys.

KATE: Yes.

PREACHER: And how many boys did you have sex with during that year?

KATE: Three.

PREACHER: You had sex with three different boys. Is that right, Kate?

KATE: Yes.

PREACHER: Tell us.

KATE: I had sex with three different boys.

PREACHER: Why'd you do it, Kate?

KATE: Because it was fun.

PREACHER: Because it was fun. Fun. She did it because it was fun. Show us the results of fun, Franky Jack.

(Slides. CF. CF's face contorted into a rictus of pain. A closeup of CF's face. Closer and closer)

PREACHER: Who's this, Kate?

KATE: My friend. Pamela.

PREACHER: Did you believe it was Pamela when you first saw her in the hospital?

KATE: No.

PREACHER: Who'd you think it was?

KATE: An old man.

PREACHER: How old is Pamela?

KATE: Sixteen.

PREACHER: How old are you, Kate?

KATE: Sixteen.

PREACHER: Do you want this to happen to you?

KATE: No.

PREACHER: What do you want?

KATE: I want to find the Lord.

(Dramatic organ music)

PREACHER: Kate Bandell. You are standing on the hilltop of your soul. Standing face to face with Jesus. And He is listening. Kate Bandell. SPEAK STRAIGHT TO JESUS!

(An intense spotlight on KATE)

KATE: Jesus. Please. Sex felt so good. I thought it was good. I didn't know that You had hidden Death into it to weed out the sinners of the world. But now I see that You have hidden death into it to weed out the sinners of the world. I'm very sorry. Please forgive me, Jesus. I won't do it anymore. Until I get married. I promise. I want to get married and have children and—

(A voice from the rear of the theater)

KATE'S FATHER: Stop this! *(He runs down the aisle.)*

KATE: No, Daddy, no, go back, Daddy, I'm gonna get sick, Daddy, no, I'll get sick—

KATE'S FATHER: You're not going to get sick, you're a healthy young girl! All this is a pack of lies. *(Into the camera)* You're going to die! You're all going to die! Whatever you do, whatever you believe, you and you and you and you are all. going. to.

(As KATE'S FATHER talks, pandemonium breaks out:)

CHOIR MEMBER: Turn off—

CHOIR MEMBER: Cut—

CHOIR MEMBER: Call—

CHOIR MEMBER: the lights—

CHOIR MEMBER: the cops—

CHOIR MEMBER: Cut the camera—

PREACHER: CUT GODDAMIT

(An abrupt blackout. Complete silence)

(KATE'S FATHER ushers KATE out of the darkness, and encourages her to approach CF's bed.)

KATE: Pammy? Listen. It's me. Kate. I'm sorry I haven't come to visit you here. I thought, they told me you were in a hospital somewhere else. And then, they convinced me that…They made me think that if I, if I stayed your friend, something very, something, like. I'm sorry. Is it okay? *(She puts her hand on CF's cheek— but her hand springs back, as it has touched something cold and hard.)*

(THE FOUR PEOPLE in their gauze masks emerge out of the darkness, and move toward KATE. She sees them.)

KATE: Go away. I'm trying to tell her something.
Go away! It isn't too late! I need to tell her something!
Go away! Get away from me! Get away!

(THE FOUR PEOPLE jump on KATE. She screams, long and hard.)

(Enter RICHARD. Lights on the hospital scene)

RICHARD: Come on. This isn't going to do anybody any good. Come on.

(RICHARD tries to pull KATE out with him. She wrenches away.)

(SHEILA cowers away, terrified of KATE.)

KATE: Say it, you know the truth, now say it!

(SHEILA stares fixedly into the seltzer bottle, tipping it this way and that. Enter MARYANNE.)

SHEILA: Maryanne! Oh, Maryanne! Oh god thank god Maryanne! Yes, we have an appointment now, don't we? Five o'clock. Well, I was just saying, there was just somebody saying, my friend, really, a friend of Paul's, a co-worker and her husband, Kate and—Richard! Richard! They were just leaving.

MARYANNE: *(Seeing* KATE*)* You.

KATE: Hi, Maryanne.

SHEILA: Do you know each other?

MARYANNE: *(With suppressed fury)* This is the young lady who comes to my lectures and heckles with the same question.

KATE: Doesn't everybody die?

MARYANNE: And how is he today, Sheila?

SHEILA: Much better! He ate a whole half banana and he didn't puke! That's why I have his T V on!

(MARYANNE *picks up the mending from a chair.)*

MARYANNE: Fixing something?

SHEILA: Oh! Another pair of jeans! It never stops, does it? Paul used to do the mending but when he comes home this time, we're going to get a sewing machine. Two little cockroaches will buy us a sewing machine, Paul! And a washing machine! And everything we need to be happy, Paul!

(MARYANNE *walks directly to* CF, *speaks to* CF *in clear, ringing tones.)*

MARYANNE: Good evening, Paul. It's I, Maryanne. I'm the hospital psychologist and I come here every evening at five o'clock. You are Paul Glass. You are an accountant. You are thirty-eight years old. You are husband to Sheila. Father to Sondra and Beverly. You are in the hospital. But you are doing fine. You are fighting the disease and if you can muster the courage and a strong, positive attitude, you will soon go home.

CF: I.

MARYANNE: Did you hear that? He said "I". Paul. Can you add one more word? I am. I am.

(CF *does not respond.*)

Well! That was great progress for today! Great progress! Great progress! Good job!

(*Exit* MARYANNE. SHEILA *speaks feverishly to* CF.)

SHEILA: I am Paul Glass! I am husband to Sheila!

RICHARD: Come on, Kate. We have to go. Now.

SHEILA: Look! Look! He's looking at me! He knows me!

RICHARD: Yes, he knows you! He hates you! You've killed him with your chatter and your chores and your cockroaches in a seltzer bottle! He has to die to escape you!

SHEILA: No that's not why he's dying! (*Claps hand to mouth. She runs offstage.*)

RICHARD: Should I go after her—

RICHARD:	KATE:
—and apologize.	Would it be okay—

KATE: —for you to leave me alone with him for a minute?

(RICHARD *exits.*)

(KATE *is alone with the* CF. *She takes a step toward his bedside, and comes face to face with* THE NURSE.)

KATE: There's something I need to say to him.

THE NURSE: Keep it brief.

(*Very slowly,* KATE *approaches* CF. *She places her hand on* CF's *cheek and* CF's *face turns toward her, like a plant that turns involuntarily, irresistibly toward the sun. She climbs into bed and takes him in her arms.*)

KATE: Paul. You are dying. And that's all right. Go now. Let go now. With peace in your heart. Everybody dies. Shhh. Shhh. Shhh.

(*Without warning,* CF *spews a great hurtle of vomit, a sickly yellow projectile that* KATE *wipes away from his mouth as she continues to go Shhh Shhh Shhh.*)

(CF *lies back in her arms, spent, and his teeth chatter involuntarily as he dies.*)

CF: K k k k k k k k k k k k k k k k k

(CF *is perfectly still now.* KATE *holds him.*)

(THE NURSE *steps forward, holding her giant syringe. She pulls the plunger as she speaks to the audience.*)

THE NURSE: You don't got to give me love. You don't got to give me salvation. You don't got to give me fame, or even a name. You just got to give me one thing, honey, one precious thing.

(*SFX: Distant cymbals clash*)

(*Streamers fall from the heavens.*)

(*Blackout*)

END OF PLAY